SEA HORSE

LIVING THINGS

SEA HORSE

Rebecca Stefoff

BENCHMARK BOOKS

MARSHALL CAVENDISH
NEW YORK

Benchmark Books
Marshall Cavendish Corporation
99 White Plains Road
Tarrytown, New York 10591-9001

Illustrations by Jean Cassels

Library of Congress Cataloging-in-Publication Data
Stefoff, Rebecca, 1951-
Sea Horse / by Rebecca Stefoff.
p.   cm. — (Living things)
Includes bibliographical references (p.   ) and index.
Summary: Describes the physical characteristics, behavior,
and camouflage abilities of this unusual fish.
ISBN 0-7614-0116-4 (lib. bdg.)
1. Sea horses—Juvenile literature. [1. Sea horses.] I. Title.
II. Series: Stefoff, Rebecca, l951-   Living things.
QL638.S9S74 1997   597' .53—dc20   96-6212 CIP   AC

Photo research by Ellen Barrett Dudley

Cover photo: *Photo Researchers, Inc.:* Mike Neumann

The photographs in this book are used by permission and through the courtesy of:
Photo Researchers, Inc.: Kjell B. Sandved, title page; Gregory Ochocki, 8;
Tom McHugh, 9, 20; Charles Angelo, 12; Fred McConnaughey, 18; Jacana, 19
(right); Dr. Paul A. Zahal, 25. *Peter Arnold:* Ikan, 6, 14 (left and right), 15 (top),
22-23, 27; Fred Bavendam, 21. *Animals, Animals:* David Fleetham, 7; Bruce
Watkins, 10 (left); Rudie H. Kuiter, 10 (right), 24, 26; Miriam Austerman, 11;
W. Gregory Brown, 13, 15 (bottom); Max Gibbs, 16-17; Zig Leszczynski, 19 (left),
20 (left), 32.

Printed in the United States of America

3   5   6   4   2

To Zachary, with thanks for all his help

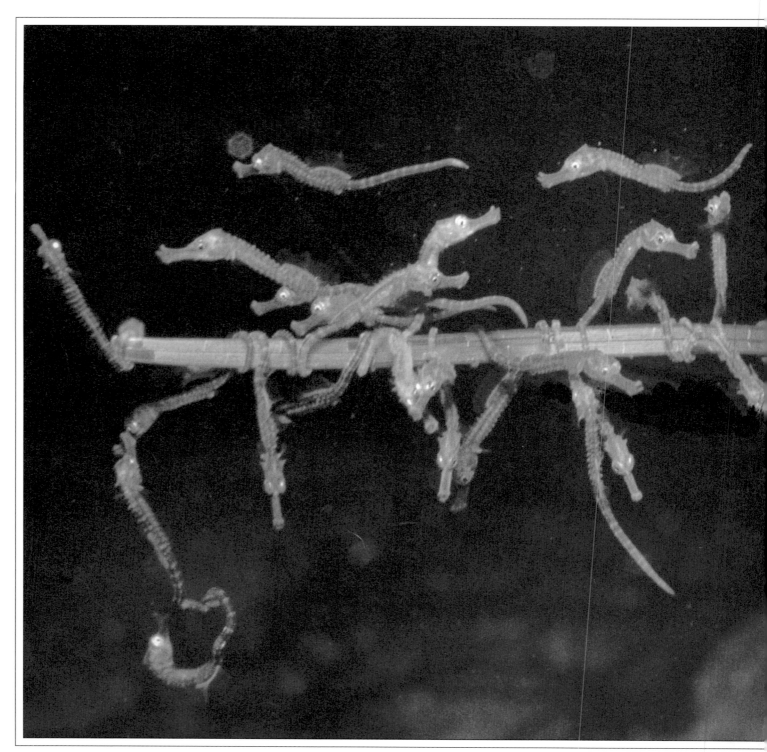

baby Atlantic sea horses

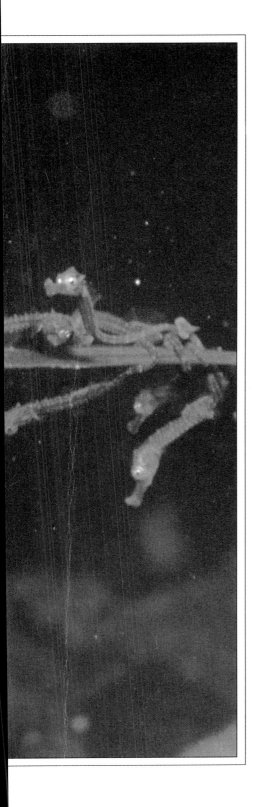

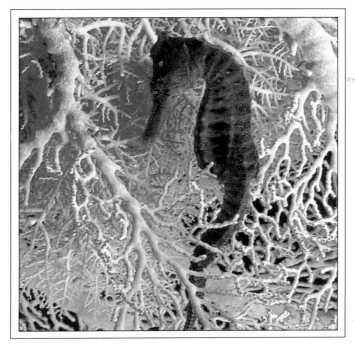

golden sea horse in fan coral

Sea horses live in the ocean, where the water is shallow and not too cold.

These baby sea horses clinging to sea grass are only a few minutes old. They are smaller than your little finger. Even the grown-up sea horse hiding in pink coral is much smaller than your hand.

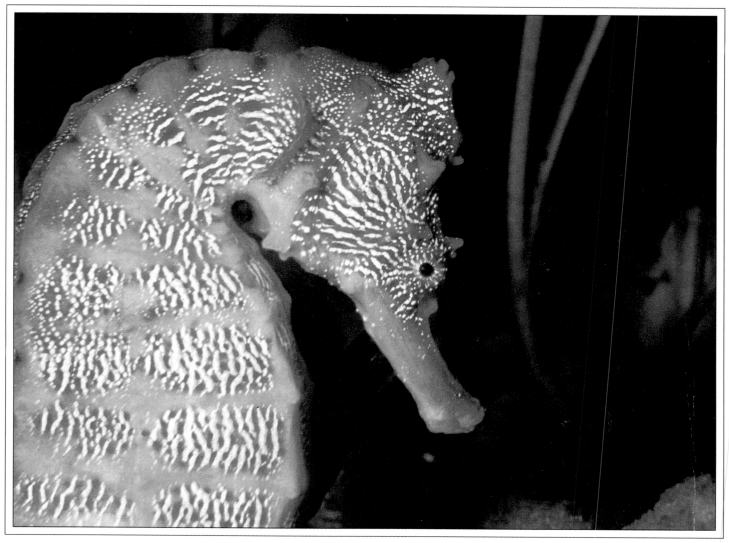

Pacific sea horse

The sea horse is a fish, but it doesn't look very much like other fish.

Some people think that the sea horse's head looks like the head of a horse. Do you think so?

close-up of a sea horse

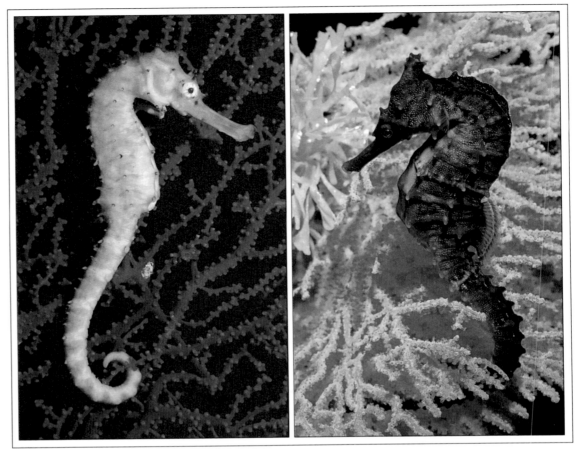

Philippine sea horse in coral　　　　*White's sea horse in coral*

Most fish swim on their stomachs, but not the sea horse. The sea horse swims standing up, and it swims v-e-r-y slowly.

Sea horses spend a lot of time standing still on their long, twisty tails. They like to hold themselves in place by wrapping their tails around grasses or corals.

Pacific sea horse

Reid's sea horse

Reid's sea horse

A sea horse's tail is surprisingly strong. It is very hard to move a sea horse that has its tail wrapped around a holdfast.

Did you know that sea horses are ticklish? The best way to loosen the sea horse's grip on its holdfast is to gently tickle its tail.

leafy sea dragons

The sea horse's closest relatives are the sea dragons and the pipefish.

The leafy sea dragon looks like a plant, but it is really a fish.

Why does it have those long, leafy-looking fins? They help it hide. When a leafy sea dragon swims into a clump of seaweed, it seems to disappear.

The pipefish is long and narrow, like a pipe. Its long snout is at the bottom of the picture. Can you find its big golden eye?

common sea dragon

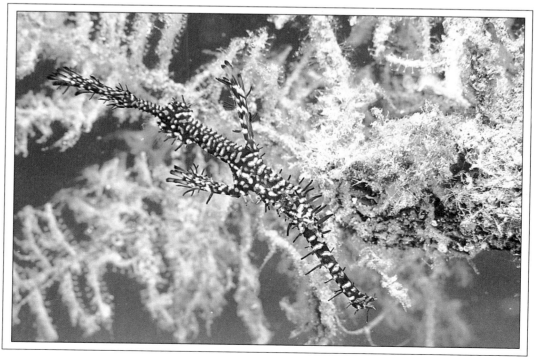

ghost pipefish

Sea horses come in many sizes and colors. The world's smallest sea horses are only half an inch tall (a little more than a centimeter) when they are full grown. The biggest sea horses are 14 inches tall (about 36 centimeters)— a little taller than this book.

Sea horses are too slow to swim away from bigger fish that might eat them. Instead, sea horses hide from their enemies. A sea horse can change its color to blend with whatever is around it. Can you spot the four sea horses in this patch of coral?

Reid's sea horses

Pacific sea horse

The sea horse's trick of matching its background is called camouflage. Two of these sea horses are using color camouflage to hide. The sea horse in the middle is trying another trick. It is hiding by pretending to be just another branch of coral.

Atlantic lined sea horse   *golden sea horse*

short-snouted sea horse with ascidians, or sea squirts

Atlantic lined sea horse

big-bellied sea horses eating

When a sea horse is frightened, it curls its tail around its snout and makes itself very small. Or it may look for a hiding place inside a clump of small animals called sea squirts.

Sea horses eat tiny shrimp and other creatures that are too small for people to see. The sea horse's long snout works like a vacuum cleaner, sucking up food from the ocean floor.

two sea horse couples

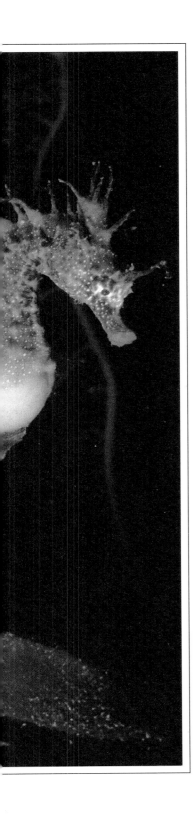

Do you see the knobs and spines on these sea horses' heads? Many sea horses have these pointy growths.

The knobs and spines are called cirri. They help the sea horse hide itself in weeds and grasses.

Sometimes cirri keep the sea horse from being eaten. Fish snap up spiny sea horses and then spit them out. Ouch! Too sharp and prickly!

White's sea horses mating

The strangest thing about the sea horse is the way it is born. Sea horses are born from their fathers, not their mothers.

Parent sea horses dance and twirl together for hours. Then the female sea horse lays her eggs in a pouch on the male's stomach.

The pouch is a safe home for the eggs as they grow into baby sea horses. The father sea horse's pouch gets bigger and bigger, until one day . . .

pregnant male short-snouted sea horses

male short-snouted sea horse giving birth

. . . the baby sea horses are ready to be born.
They swim out of their father's pouch and wrap their
tails around the first thing they see.

The tiny sea horses link tails and spin around and
around, taking their first look at the big new world
outside their father's pouch. After a few hours
together, they will separate. Each little sea horse will
go its own way, ready for life under the ocean's
waves.

baby sea horses

A QUICK LOOK AT THE SEA HORSE

Sea horses, sea dragons, and pipefish are all members of the pipefish family. All of the fish in this family have tube-shaped snouts. Their bodies are covered with stiff, bony plates or rings instead of being covered with scales like most other fish.

Here are six kinds of sea horses along with their scientific names in Latin and a few key facts.

DWARF SEA HORSE

Hippocampus zosterae
(hip oh CAMP us ZOSS ter eye)
A common sea horse in the Gulf of Mexico and the Caribbean Sea. Has short, stiff cirri, or spiny growths, on its head. Usually pale yellow in color. About an inch long (2.5 cm).

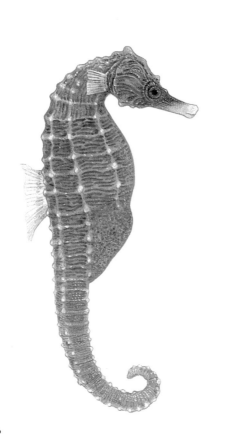

ATLANTIC LINED SEA HORSE

Hippocampus erectus
(hip oh CAMP us eh RECK tus)
Most common sea horse along the Atlantic coast of North America. Generally tan, with white and black horizontal stripes. Measures about eight inches in length (20 cm).

NEW CALEDONIAN SEA HORSE

Hippocampus bargibanti
(hip oh CAMP us bar geh BAN tee)
World's smallest sea horse. Measures half an inch long (1 cm) when fully grown. Found only off the coast of New Caledonia, an island in the South Pacific Ocean not far from Australia.

BIG-BELLIED SEA HORSE

Hippocampus abdominalis
(hip oh CAMP us ab dom in AL us)
Measures ten inches in length (25 cm) and has a large stomach. Has long cirri on its head and dark spots on its back and sides. Lives near New Zealand and southern Australia.

SHORT-SNOUTED SEA HORSE

Hippocampus breviceps
(hip oh CAMP us BREV eh seps)
Two to three inches long (5-7.5 cm), with a plump belly. Has long cirri, or growths, on its head and spine. Lives off the southern coast of Australia.

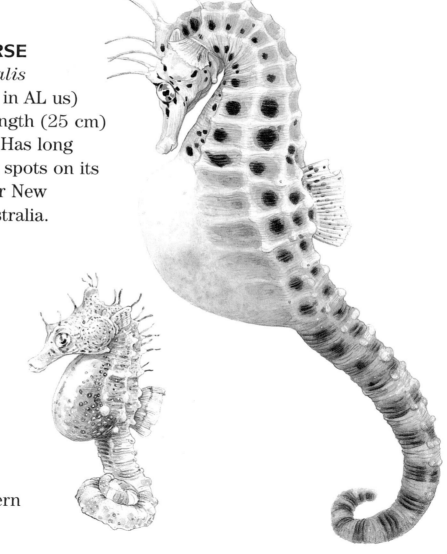

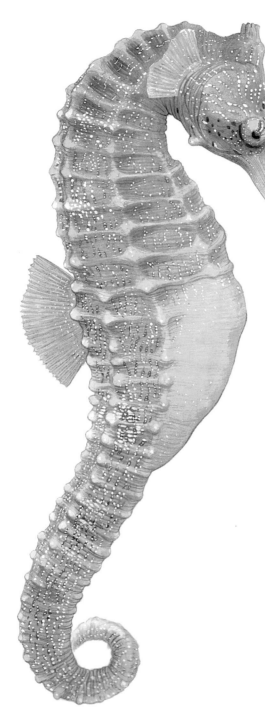

PACIFIC SEA HORSE

Hippocampus ingens
(hip oh CAMP us in guns)
World's largest sea horse. Can measure fourteen inches (35 cm) from tip of snout to tip of tail. Lives in Pacific waters off the coast of the Americas from California to the Equator.

Taking Care of the Sea Horse

Many sea horses are in danger. Water pollution poisons their food, and fishing disturbs or destroys their homes. Each year, millions of sea horses are caught in nets and dried in the sun. In some countries, they are made into souvenirs or ground into powders that are used as medicines. Scientists who study ocean life say that some kinds of sea horses may disappear because people are capturing too many of them.

Sea horses need clean oceans and safe, quiet shorelines to live. Their future is in our hands.

Find Out More

Brown, Anne Ensign. *Wonders of Sea Horses*. New York: Dodd, Mead, 1979.

Morris, Robert A. *Seahorse*. New York: Harper & Row, 1972.

Index

Rebecca Stefoff has published many books for young readers. Science and environmental issues are among her favorite subjects. She lives in Oregon and enjoys observing the natural world while hiking, camping, and scuba diving.

Atlantic lined sea horse